KWANZAA

Sarah Cords

DiscoverRoo
An Imprint of Pop!
popbooksonline.com

abdobooks.com

Published by Pop!, a division of ABDO, PO Box 398166, Minneapolis, Minnesota 55439. Copyright © 2021 by POP, LLC. International copyrights reserved in all countries. No part of this book may be reproduced in any form without written permission from the publisher. Pop!™ is a trademark and logo of POP, LLC.

Printed in the United States of America, North Mankato, Minnesota.

052020
092020

THIS BOOK CONTAINS RECYCLED MATERIALS

Cover Photo: Purestock/Alamy
Interior Photos: Purestock/Alamy, 1; Sarah A. Miller/Tyler Morning Telegraph/AP Images, 5; Shutterstock Images, 6; iStockphoto, 7, 13, 14, 15, 16 (bottom), 17 (top), 19, 23, 26, 27, 28, 29, 30; Shutterstock Images, 9; Library of Congress, 10; AP Images, 11, 12, 22; Terrence Jennings/Polaris/Newscom, 16 (top); John Mutrux/KRT/Newscom, 17; Jennifer Szymaszek/AP Images, 20–21, 31; Alida Latham/DanitaDelimont.com/Danita Delimont Photography/Newscom, 25

Editor: Connor Stratton
Series Designer: Jake Slavik

Content Consultant: Christel N. Temple, PhD, Associate Professor of Africana Studies, University of Pittsburgh

Library of Congress Control Number: 2019954995

Publisher's Cataloging-in-Publication Data

Names: Cords, Sarah, author.

Title: Kwanzaa / by Sarah Cords.

Description: Minneapolis, Minnesota : POP!, 2021 | Series: Cultural celebrations | Includes online resources and index.

Identifiers: ISBN 9781532167690 (lib. bdg.) | ISBN 9781532168796 (ebook)

Subjects: LCSH: Kwanzaa--Juvenile literature. | African Americans--Social life and customs--Juvenile literature. | Holidays--Juvenile literature. | Social customs--Juvenile literature.

Classification: DDC 394.2612--dc23

WELCOME TO DiscoverRoo!

Pop open this book and you'll find QR codes loaded with information, so you can learn even more!

Scan this code* and others like it while you read, or visit the website below to make this book pop!

popbooksonline.com/kwanzaa

*Scanning QR codes requires a web-enabled smart device with a QR code reader app and a camera.

TABLE OF
CONTENTS

CHAPTER 1
LIGHTING THE KINARA

On December 26, a family gathers for the first day of Kwanzaa. The parents help the kids light a candle in a candleholder known as a kinara. Family members

WATCH A VIDEO HERE!

A kinara holds seven candles.

exchange handmade gifts. A grandfather

tells stories about the family's history.

People often eat groundnut stew, a dish from West Africa, during Kwanzaa.

Kwanzaa happens from December 26 through January 1. Many African Americans celebrate Kwanzaa. The holiday honors black communities and **cultures**. It also celebrates what African

people have in common. This idea is

known as **Pan-Africanism**.

Kwanzaa celebrations can also include foods from East Africa, such as injera. This Ethiopian bread is flat, spongy, and tangy.

DID YOU KNOW?

Kwanzaa is a cultural holiday. It is not based on a religion.

CHAPTER 2
HISTORY OF KWANZAA

In the 1400s, Europeans began forcing

African people into **slavery**. Traders

kidnapped African people from their

homes in West Africa. The traders

sold the kidnapped Africans to white

LEARN MORE HERE!

European-American families. By 1860, white people had enslaved nearly four million African people.

Traders used guns, force, and violence to kidnap African people. These traders worked for white American and white European businesses.

DID YOU KNOW? White American laws forced Africans to work for white families without being paid.

Members of the civil rights movement used peaceful protests to take a stand against racial segregation in public places.

Enslavement in the United States ended after the Civil War (1861–1865). But African Americans still had to survive. Unequal laws and **racist** Americans made life harder for them. In the 1960s, many African Americans took part in the

civil rights movement. They called for equal treatment. Some groups found new ways to help African Americans feel proud of their **culture**.

Some civil rights groups were known as Black Freedom groups. These groups based their beliefs on the ideas of thinkers such as Malcolm X.

One of these groups was called

the US Organization. Maulana Karenga

helped form this group. Karenga believed

that African ideas and traditions were

Maulana Karenga (seated, with sunglasses) and other black leaders speak with reporters in July 1968.

Kwanzaa is based on many African traditions. One tradition is a Zulu harvest festival. The Zulu people live in South Africa.

important to remember. He wanted

African Americans to connect to those

roots again. So, he started Kwanzaa

in 1966.

The name Kwanzaa *is based on the Swahili phrase* matunda ya kwanza. *It means "first fruits."*

By the 1980s, more communities in

the United States and the world learned

how to celebrate Kwanzaa. Businesses

helped to make Kwanzaa even more popular. For example, people could buy Kwanzaa cards at the store. They could give these cards to friends and family.

Jollof rice is a popular Kwanzaa food. It's often served with chicken and fried plantains.

KWANZAA TIMELINE

1965
Maulana Karenga and Hakim Jamal found the US Organization to support black Americans.

1966
People celebrate the first Kwanzaa in Los Angeles, California.

1985
Cedric McClester publishes a popular guidebook for Kwanzaa.

1997

The US government recognizes Kwanzaa for the first time. The US Postal Service issues the first Kwanzaa stamp.

2008

The first major film about Kwanzaa comes out. It is called *The Black Candle*.

1999

The Smithsonian Institution in Washington, DC, holds its first all-day Kwanzaa celebration.

CHAPTER 3
THE SEVEN PRINCIPLES

Kwanzaa celebrates seven principles.

A principle is a main idea for people to

follow. Kwanzaa's first principle is about

people coming together. The second

is that people should be in charge of

COMPLETE AN ACTIVITY HERE!

their own lives. The third and fourth are

about people working together, both in a

business and at home.

People light candles to remember the seven principles.

DID YOU KNOW?

The seven principles of Kwanzaa are known as the Nguzo Saba.

The fifth idea says that the lives of

African American people are valuable.

Kwanzaa's sixth principle says African

YORUBA

*Learning and performing traditional music and dance
is one way people honor their culture.*

American people should be creative.

The last idea says they should believe in

themselves and their **culture**.

Each day of Kwanzaa, people light one kinara candle. Each candle stands for one of the principles. The candles have other meanings too. Three candles are red. Red stands for blood, or challenges. Three candles are green. Green stands for Africa's land. It means hope. One candle is black. This candle stands for African people.

Kinara colors are based on a Black Freedom group's Pan-African flag. Marcus Garvey led this group and created the flag.

SEVEN PRINCIPLES OF KWANZAA

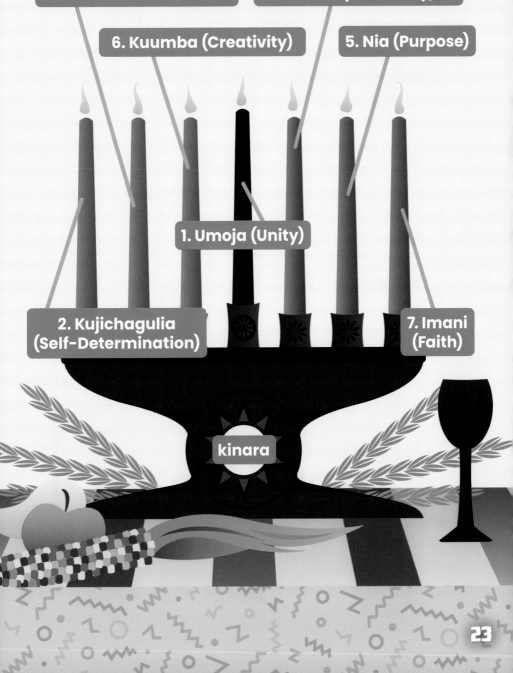

4. Ujamaa (Cooperative Economics)

3. Ujima (Collective Work and Responsibility)

6. Kuumba (Creativity)

5. Nia (Purpose)

1. Umoja (Unity)

2. Kujichagulia (Self-Determination)

7. Imani (Faith)

kinara

CHAPTER 4
THE SEVEN SYMBOLS

Many people celebrate Kwanzaa at home. Families often display the seven **symbols** in their homes. One symbol is known as the mkeka. This mat stands for

LEARN MORE HERE!

African history and **culture**. People place

the other symbols on the mat.

Adinkra symbols stand for wise sayings. People in West Africa often use them to decorate clothing.

DID YOU KNOW?

During Kwanzaa, some people wear clothes with African fabric or designs, such as adinkra symbols.

KARAMU

On December 31, families and friends have a karamu. This is a big feast. People make traditional African dishes. One example is zom. It is a spinach and meat dish from Central Africa. Music is another important part of a karamu. People play music and beat drums. They dance.

Crops are one of these symbols. They stand for African harvest festivals. Corn is a third symbol. Ears of corn stand for

Sweet potato pie is often served as dessert during a karamu.

children. They provide hope for the future.

The unity cup is a fourth symbol. People

drink from this cup. It stands for people

coming together.

The kinara and candles are two more symbols of Kwanzaa. The last symbol is known as zawadi. These are gifts people give to one another. People often give gifts to elders. Respecting older family members is an important part of the holiday.

Popular gifts at Kwanzaa include books.

Family members may get together to cook a big meal.

MAKING CONNECTIONS

TEXT-TO-SELF

Kwanzaa celebrates seven principles. What values or ideas are important to you and your family?

TEXT-TO-TEXT

Have you read books about other holidays? What do they have in common with Kwanzaa? How are they different?

TEXT-TO-WORLD

Kwanzaa has seven symbols. Can you think of symbols that are associated with other holidays?

GLOSSARY

civil rights movement – a struggle in the 1950s and 1960s that involved people working to gain equal rights for African Americans.

culture – the ideas, lifestyle, and traditions of a group of people.

Pan-Africanism – a belief that all people with African backgrounds should come together.

racist – having to do with hatred of or bad treatment of people because of their race.

slavery – a system where certain people are owned by other people.

symbol – something that stands for something else because of certain similarities.

INDEX

ONLINE RESOURCES
popbooksonline.com

Scan this code* and others like it while you read, or visit the website below to make this book pop!

popbooksonline.com/kwanzaa

*Scanning QR codes requires a web-enabled smart device with a QR code reader app and a camera.